FAVOURITE WORSHIP SONGS

50 Easy-to-play arrangements
for keyboard and guitar

FAVOURITE WORSHIP SONGS

50 Easy-to-play arrangements
for keyboard and guitar

We hope you enjoy the music in this book. Further copies are available
from your local music shop or Christian bookshop.

In case of difficulty, please contact the publisher direct by writing to:

The Sales Department
KEVIN MAYHEW LTD
Buxhall
Stowmarket
Suffolk IP14 3BW

Phone 01449 737978
Fax 01449 737834
E-mail info@kevinmayhewltd.com

Please ask for our complete catalogue of outstanding Church Music.

First published in Great Britain in 1996 by Kevin Mayhew Ltd.

This edition © Copyright 1998 Kevin Mayhew Ltd.

ISBN 1 84003 224 3
ISMN M 57004 411 5
Catalogue No: 1450102

1 2 3 4 5 6 7 8 9

Front cover illustration by Karen Perrins
Cover design by Jaquetta Sergeant

Compiled by Jonathan Bugden
Music arrangements by Christopher Tambling and Donald Thomson.
Music Editor: Donald Thomson

Printed and bound in Great Britain

Contents

ALL HAIL THE LAMB

All hail the lamb, en-throned on high:

his praise shall be our bat-tle-cry:

he reigns vic-to-ri-ous, for-e-ver glo-ri-ous,

his name is Je-sus, he is the Lord.

Words and music: Dave Bilbrough

REJOICE!

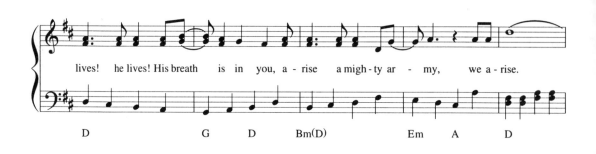

claim.   He rides in ma-jes-ty to lead us in-to

D   A7   Bm(D)

D.S.

vic-to-ry;   the world shall see that Christ is Lord!   Re -

G   Bm(D)   Em   A

2. God is at work in us
   his purpose to perform,
   building a kingdom
   of power, not of words,
   where things impossible,
   by faith, shall be made possible;
   let's give the glory
   to him now.

3. Though we are weak, his grace
   is everything we need;
   we're made of clay
   but this treasure is within.
   He turns our weaknesses
   into his opportunities,
   so that the glory
   goes to him.

Words and music: Graham Kendrick

I BELIEVE IN JESUS

2. I believe in you, Lord;
   I believe you are the Son of God.
   I believe you died and rose again,
   I believe you paid for us all.
   And I believe you're here now,
   standing in our midst.
   Here with the power to heal now,
   and the grace to forgive.

Words and music: Marc Nelson

BE BOLD, BE STRONG

Words and music: Morris Chapman

MEEKNESS AND MAJESTY

Majestically

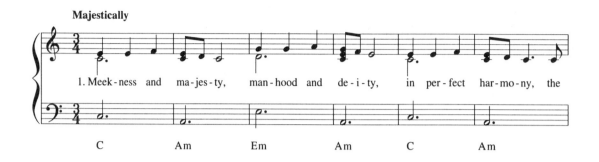

1. Meek-ness and ma-jes-ty, man-hood and de-i-ty, in per-fect har-mo-ny, the

C   Am   Em   Am   C   Am

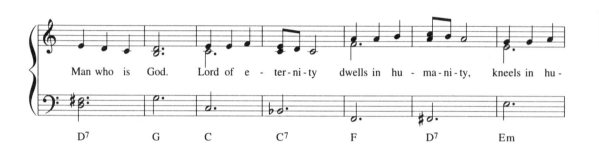

Man who is God. Lord of e-ter-ni-ty dwells in hu-ma-ni-ty, kneels in hu-

D⁷   G   C   C⁷   F   D⁷   Em

Refrain

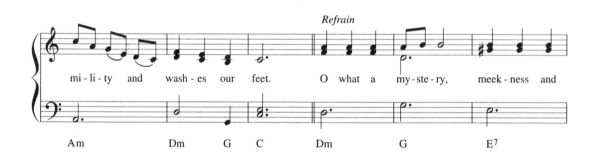

mi-li-ty and wash-es our feet. O what a my-ste-ry, meek-ness and

Am   Dm   G   C   Dm   G   E⁷

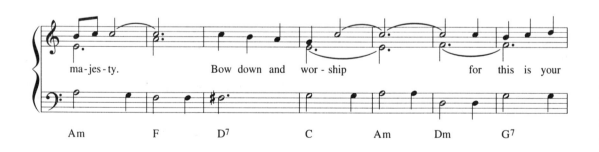

ma-jes-ty. Bow down and wor-ship for this is your

Am   F   D⁷   C   Am   Dm   G⁷

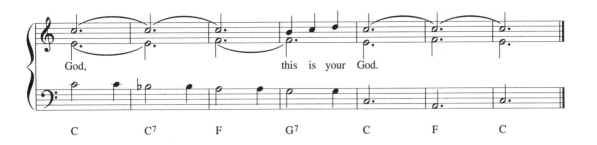

God,   this is your God.

C   C7   F   G7   C   F   C

2. Father's pure radiance,
   perfect in innocence,
   yet learns obedience
   to death on a cross.
   Suffering to give us life,
   conquering through sacrifice,
   and as they crucify
   prays: 'Father, forgive.'

3. Wisdom unsearchable,
   God the invisible,
   love indestructable
   in frailty appears.
   Lord of infinity,
   stooping so tenderly,
   lifts our humanity
   to the heights of his throne.

Words and music: Graham Kendrick

YOU LAID ASIDE YOUR MAJESTY

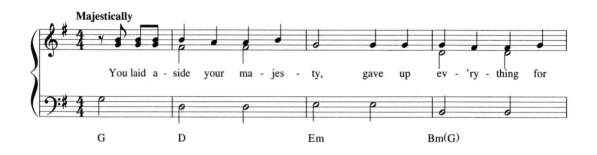

You laid a - side your ma - jes - ty, gave up ev - 'ry - thing for

G   D   Em   Bm(G)

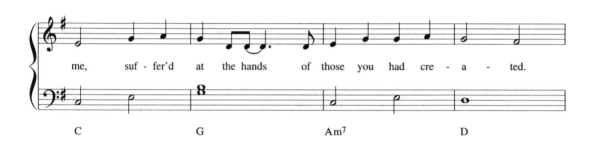

me, suf - fer'd at the hands of those you had cre - a - ted.

C   G   Am⁷   D

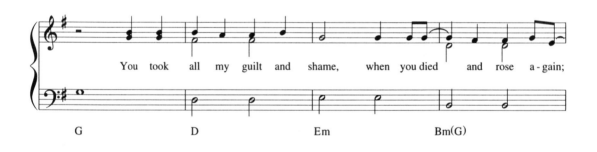

You took all my guilt and shame, when you died and rose a - gain;

G   D   Em   Bm(G)

now to - day you reign, in heav'n and earth ex - al - ted.

C   G   Am⁷   D

Words and music: Noel Richards

JESUS PUT THIS SONG INTO OUR HEARTS

2. Jesus taught us how to live in harmony,
   Jesus taught us how to live in harmony,
   different faces, different races, he made us one,
   Jesus taught us how to live in harmony.

3. Jesus taught us how to be a family,
   Jesus taught us how to be a family,
   loving one another with the love that he gives,
   Jesus taught us how to be a family.

4. Jesus turned our sorrows into dancing,
   Jesus turned our sorrows into dancing,
   changed our tears of sadness into rivers of joy,
   Jesus turned our sorrows into a dance.

5. *Instrumental*

Words and music: Graham Kendrick

PURIFY MY HEART
Refiner's Fire

Words and music: Brian Doerksen

THERE IS POWER IN THE NAME OF JESUS

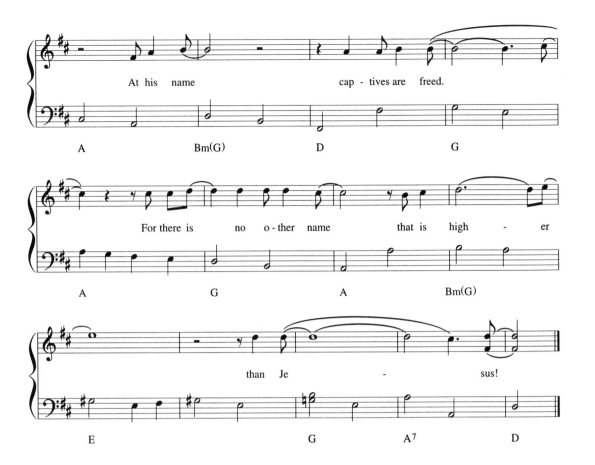

At his name cap - tives are freed.

A   Bm(G)   D   G

For there is no o - ther name that is high - er

A   G   A   Bm(G)

than Je - sus!

E   G   A⁷   D

2. There is power in the name of Jesus,
like a sword in our hands.
We declare in the name of Jesus;
we shall stand! we shall stand!
At his name God's enemies
shall be crushed beneath our feet.
For there is no other name that is higher
than Jesus!

Words and music: Noel Richards

FROM HEAVEN YOU CAME

The Servant King

Worshipfully

1. From heav'n you came, help-less babe, en-tered our world, your

*Capo 5

Dm / Am   A / E   B♭ / F   C / G   F / C

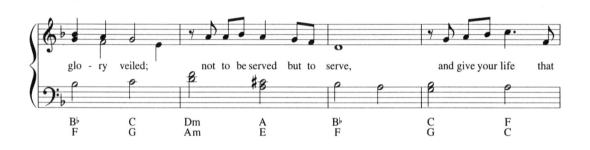

glo-ry veiled; not to be served but to serve, and give your life that

B♭ / F   C / G   Dm / Am   A / E   B♭ / F   C / G   F / C

Refrain

we might live. This is our God, the Ser-vant King, he calls us

B♭ / F   C / G   F / C   C / G   Dm / Am   F / C

now to fol-low him, to bring our lives as a dai-ly of-fer-

Gm / Dm   B♭ / F   F / C   C / G   F / C

* Alternative capo chords for guitar

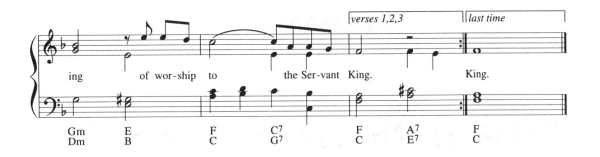

ing of wor-ship to the Ser-vant King. King.

verses 1,2,3 | *last time*

Gm | E | F | C⁷ | F | A⁷ | F
Dm | B | C | G⁷ | C | E⁷ | C

2. There in the garden of tears,
   my heavy load he chose to bear;
   his heart with sorrow was torn,
   'Yet not my will but yours', he said.

3. Come, see his hands and his feet,
   and scars that speak of sacrifice,
   hands that flung stars into space
   to cruel nails surrendered.

4. So let us learn how to serve,
   and in our lives enthrone him;
   each other's needs to prefer,
   for it is Christ we're serving.

Words and music: Graham Kendrick

HOSANNA

1. Ho-san-na, ho-san-na, ho-san-na in the high - est! Ho-san - na, ho-san - na, ho-san-na in the high - est! Lord, we lift up your name, with hearts full of praise; be ex-alt-ed, O Lord, my God! Ho-san-na in the high - est!

2. Glory, glory, glory to the King of kings!
   Glory, glory, glory to the King of kings!
   Lord, we lift up your name,
   with hearts full of praise;
   be exalted, O Lord, my God!
   Glory to the King of kings!

Words and music: Carl Tuttle

AS THE DEER

2. I want you more than gold or silver,
   only you can satisfy.
   You alone are the real joy-giver
   and the apple of my eye.

3. You're my friend and you're my brother,
   even though you are a king.
   I love you more than any other,
   so much more than anything.

Words and music: Martin Nystrom

JESUS SHALL TAKE THE HIGHEST HONOUR

With strength

Je-sus shall take the high-est hon-our, Je-sus shall take the high-est praise: let all earth join heav'n in ex-alt-ing the name which is a-bove all o-ther names. Let's bow the knee in hum-ble a-do-ra-tion, for at his name ev-'ry knee must bow. Let ev-'ry tongue con-fess he is Christ, God's on-ly Son.

Words and music: Chris Bowater

GREAT IS THE LORD

Words and music: Steve McEwan

FATHER GOD I WONDER

I will sing your praises

Words and music: Ian Smale

BE STILL, FOR THE PRESENCE OF THE LORD

2. Be still, for the glory of the Lord is shining all around;
   he burns with holy fire, with splendour he is crowned.
   How awesome is the sight, our radiant king of light!
   Be still, for the glory of the Lord, is shining all around.

3. Be still, for the power of the Lord is moving in this place,
   he comes to cleanse and heal, to minister his grace.
   No work too hard for him, in faith receive from him;
   be still, for the power of the Lord is moving in this place.

Words and music: David J Evans

I AM A NEW CREATION

and I will sing of all that you have done.

C   Am   F   G

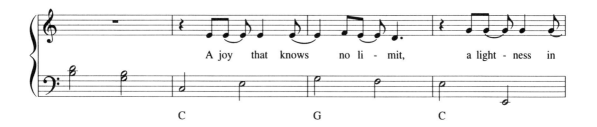

A joy that knows no li - mit, a light - ness in

C   G   C

my spi - rit, here in the grace of God I stand.

F   C   F   G   C   F   C

Words and music: Dave Bilbrough

MAJESTY

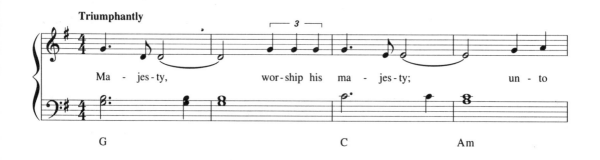

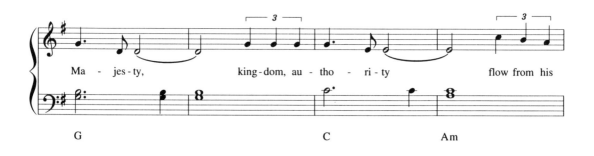

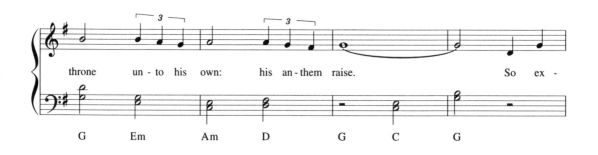

Words and music: Jack W Hayford

GIVE THANKS WITH A GRATEFUL HEART

what the Lord has done for us. Give us. Give thanks.

Em   F   Dsus⁴ D Dsus⁴ D G

Words and music: Henry Smith

SUCH LOVE

Flowing

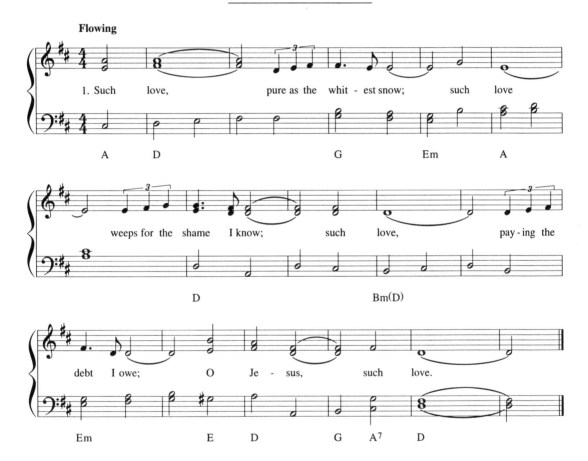

1. Such love, pure as the whit - est snow; such love

A D   G Em A

weeps for the shame I know; such love, pay - ing the

D   Bm(D)

debt I owe; O Je - sus, such love.

Em E D G A⁷ D

2. Such love, stilling my restlessness;
   such love, filling my emptiness;
   such love, showing me holiness;
   O Jesus, such love.

3. Such love springs from eternity;
   such love, streaming through history;
   such love, fountain of life to me;
   O Jesus, such love.

Words and music: Graham Kendrick

COME ON AND CELEBRATE

Words and music: Dave Bankhead and Patricia Morgan

ALL HEAVEN DECLARES

Majestically

1. All heav'n declares the glory of the risen Lord.
Who can compare with the beauty of the Lord?
Forever he will be the Lamb upon the throne.
I gladly bow the knee and worship him alone.

2. I will proclaim
    the glory of the risen Lord.
    Who once was slain
    to reconcile man to God.
    Forever you will be
    the Lamb upon the throne.
    I gladly bow the knee
    and worship you alone.

Words and music: Noel and Tricia Richards

JESUS, WE CELEBRATE YOUR VICTORY

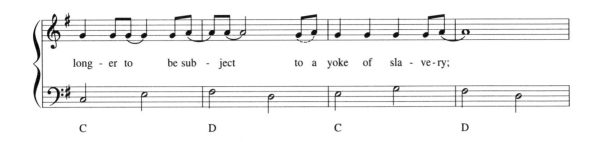

long - er to be sub - ject to a yoke of sla - ve-ry;

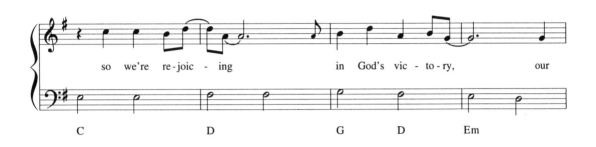

so we're re - joic - ing in God's vic - to - ry, our

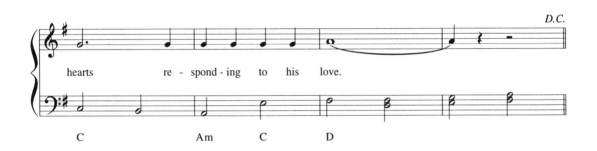

D.C.

hearts re - spond - ing to his love.

2. His Spirit in us releases us from fear,
   the way to him is open, with boldness we draw near.
   And in his presence our problems disappear;
   our hearts responding to his love.

Words and music: John Gibson

39

TO BE IN YOUR PRESENCE

2. To rest in your presence,
   not rushing away.
   To cherish each moment,
   here I would stay.

Words and music: Noel Richards

THERE IS A REDEEMER

Hymn-like

1. There is a Re-deem-er, Je-sus, God's own Son,

D G D Em A⁷ D A

pre-cious Lamb of God, Mes-si-ah, Ho-ly One.

D G Em A⁷ D

Refrain

Thank you, O my Fa-ther, for giv-ing us your Son, and

G D G A D A

leav-ing your Spi-rit till the work on earth is done.

D G Em A⁷ D

2. Jesus my Redeemer,
   Name above all names,
   precious Lamb of God, Messiah,
   O for sinners slain.

3. When I stand in glory
   I will see his face.
   And there I'll serve my King for ever,
   in that holy place.

Words and music: Melody Green

AMAZING LOVE

death he dies, that I might live, that

D Am7 D

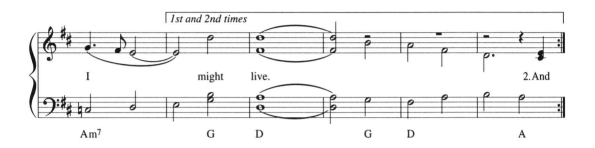

1st and 2nd times

I might live. 2.And

Am7 G D G D A

3rd time

might live, that I might live.

D Am7 G D

2. And so they watched him die,
   despised, rejected;
   but oh the blood he shed
   flowed for me!

3. And now this love of Christ
   shall flow like rivers;
   come wash your guilt away,
   live again!

Words and music: Graham Kendrick

WE WANT TO SEE JESUS LIFTED HIGH

We want to see Je - sus lif - ted high, a ban - ner that flies a - cross this land,

G   D   Em   C

that all men might see the truth and know he is the way to hea - ven.

G   D   Em   C

We want to see, we want to see, we want to see Je - sus lif - ted high.
We're gon - na see, we're gon - na see, we're gon - na see Je - sus lif - ted high.

G   Em   C

We want to see, we want to see, we want to see Je - sus lif - ted high.
We're gon - na see, we're gon - na see, we're gon - na see Je - sus lif - ted high.

G   Em   C

Step by step we're mov - ing for - ward, lit - tle by

lit - tle tak - ing ground, ev - 'ry pray'r a pow - er - ful wea - pon, strong - holds

come tum - bl - ing down and down and down and down.

Words and music: Doug Horley

ALL I ONCE HELD DEAR

Knowing you

Smoothly

1. All I once held dear, built my life u-pon, all this world re-veres and wars to own, all I once thought gain I have coun-ted loss; spent and worth-less now, com-pared to this.

Refrain

Know-ing you, Je-sus, know-ing you, there is no great-er thing. You're my all, you're the best, you're my joy, my right-eous-ness, and I love you, Lord.

To verses 2. Now my

Last time love you, Lord.

2. Now my heart's desire
   is to know you more,
   to be found in you
   and known as yours.
   To possess by faith
   what I could not earn,
   all-surpassing gift
   of righteousness.

3. Oh, to know the power
   of your risen life,
   and to know you in
   your sufferings.
   To become like you
   in your death, my Lord,
   so with you to live
   and never die.

Words and music: Graham Kendrick

LORD, I LIFT YOUR NAME ON HIGH

You came from heaven to earth

Words and music: Rick Founds

LORD, THE LIGHT OF YOUR LOVE

Shine, Jesus, Shine

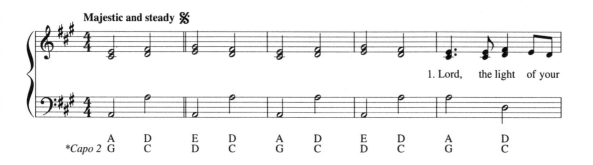

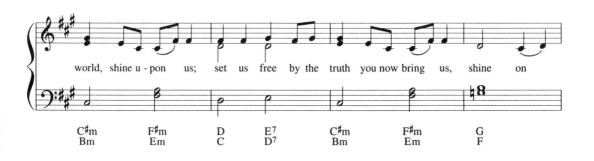

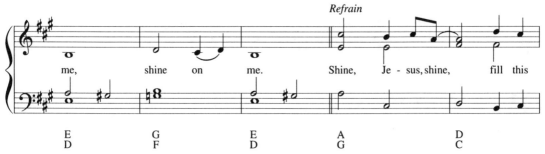

*Alternative capo chords for guitar

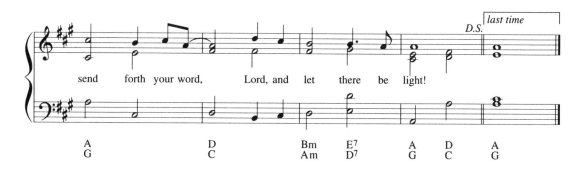

2. Lord, I come to your awesome presence,
from the shadows into your radiance;
by the blood I may enter your brightness,
search me, try me, consume all my darkness,
shine on me, shine on me.

3. As we gaze on your kingly brightness
so our faces display your likeness,
ever changing from glory to glory,
mirrored here may our lives tell your story,
shine on me, shine on me.

Words and music: Graham Kendrick

ABBA, FATHER, LET ME BE

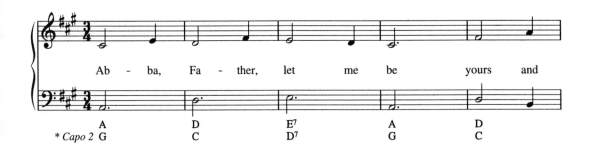

Ab - ba, Fa - ther, let me be yours and

A   D   E⁷   A   D
* *Capo 2* G   C   D⁷   G   C

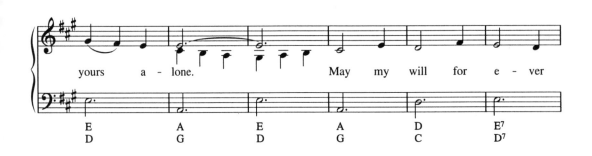

yours a - lone. May my will for e - ver

E   A   E   A   D   E⁷
D   G   D   G   C   D⁷

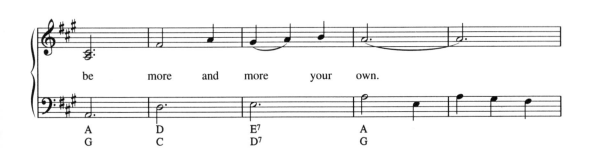

be more and more your own.

A   D   E⁷   A
G   C   D⁷   G

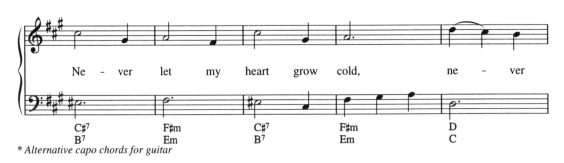

Ne - ver let my heart grow cold, ne - ver

C#⁷   F#m   C#⁷   F#m   D
B⁷   Em   B⁷   Em   C

* *Alternative capo chords for guitar*

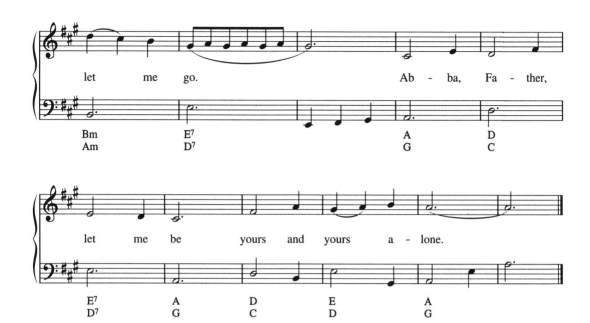

let me go. Ab - ba, Fa - ther,

Bm　　　　E⁷　　　　　　　　　　A　　　　D
Am　　　　D⁷　　　　　　　　　　G　　　　C

let me be yours and yours a - lone.

E⁷　　　A　　　D　　　E　　　A
D⁷　　　G　　　C　　　D　　　G

Words and music: Dave Bilbrough

FATHER OF CREATION

Let your glory fall

* *Alternative capo chords for guitar*

2. Ruler of the nations,
   the world has yet to see
   the full release of your promise,
   the church in victory.

   Turn to us, Lord, and touch us,
   make us strong in your might.
   Overcome our weakness,
   that we could stand up and fight.

Words and music: David Ruis

I COULD SING UNENDING SONGS

The happy song

O, I could sing un-end-ing songs of how you saved my soul. Well, I could dance a thou-sand miles be-cause of your great love.

My heart is burst-ing, Lord, to tell of all you've done. Of how you changed my life and wiped a-way the past. I wan-na shout it out, from ev'ry roof-top sing.

For now I know that God is for me, not a-gainst me. Ev-'ry-bo-dy's sing-ing now,

Asus[2] E B A

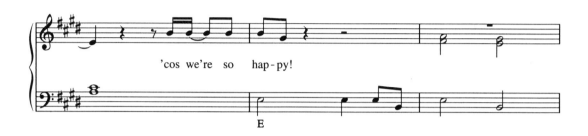

'cos we're so hap-py!

E

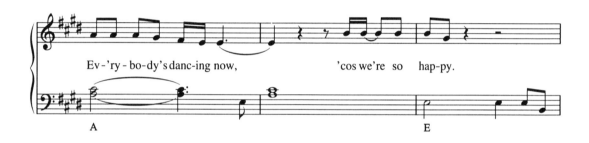

Ev-'ry-bo-dy's danc-ing now, 'cos we're so hap-py.

A E

If on-ly we could see your face and see you smi-ling o-ver us and

F#m A

D.S.

un-seen an-gels ce-le-brate, for joy is in this place! O,

F#m A E

Words and music: Martin Smith

JESUS CHRIST

Once again

2. Now you are exalted to the highest place,
   King of the heavens, where one day I'll bow.
   But for now I marvel at this saving grace,
   and I'm full of praise once again,
   I'm full of praise once again.

Words and music: Matt Redman

MY JESUS, MY SAVIOUR

Shout to the Lord

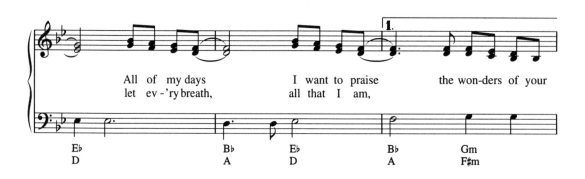

* Alternative capo chords for guitar

to the King. Moun-tains bow down and the seas will roar at the
- ver I'll stand. No - thing com-pares to the pro -

| Eb | | Fsus^4 | F | Gm | | | Eb |
| D | | Esus^4 | E | F#m | | | D |

sound of your name.
- mise I have in you.

| F | | Gm | F | Eb | F | Bb | Bbsus^4 Bb |
| E | | F#m | E | D | E | A | Asus^4 A |

Words and music: Darlene Zschech

THESE ARE THE DAYS

Days of Elijah

Words and music: Robin Mark

GREAT IS THE DARKNESS

Come, Lord Jesus

Growing in strength

1. Great is the dark - ness that cov - ers the earth, op - pres - sion, in - jus - tice and pain.

Na - tions are slip - ping in hope - less des - pair, though many have come in your name.

Watch - ing while sa - ni - ty dies, touched by the mad - ness and lies.

Refrain

Come, Lord Je - sus, come, Lord Je - sus, pour out your Spi - rit, we pray.

Come, Lord Je - sus, come, Lord Je - sus,

pour out your Spi - rit on us to - day.

to verses · *last time*

2. May now your church rise with power and love,
   this glorious gospel proclaim.
   In ev'ry nation salvation will come
   to those who believe in your name.
   Help us bring light to this world
   that we might speed your return.

3. Great celebrations on that final day
   when out of the heavens you come.
   Darkness will vanish, all sorrow will end,
   and rulers will bow at your throne.
   Our great commission complete,
   then face to face we shall meet.

Words and music: Noel Richards and Gerald Coates

ONLY BY GRACE

Words and music: Gerrit Gustafson

MAKE WAY, MAKE WAY

1. Make way, make way, for Christ the King in splen - dour ar-

rives; fling wide the gates and wel - come him in - to your

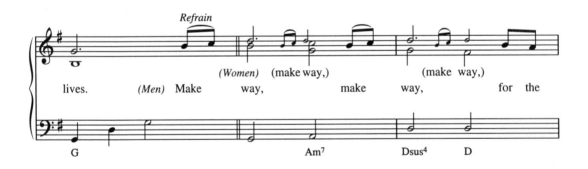

lives. *(Men)* Make way, make way, for the

(Women) (make way,) (make way,)

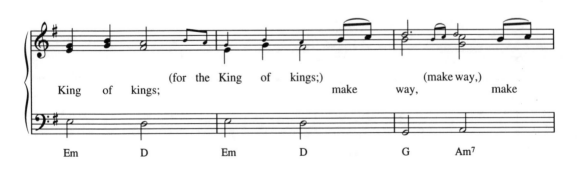

King of kings; make way, make

(for the King of kings;) (make way,)

way, (make way,) (All) and let his king - dom in!

Dsus⁴   D   Em   Dsus⁴   D⁷   G   C   G

2. He comes the broken hearts to heal,
    the pris'ners to free;
    the deaf shall hear, the lame shall dance,
    the blind shall see.

3. And those who mourn with heavy hearts,
    who weep and sigh,
    with laughter, joy and royal crown
    he'll beautify.

4. We call you now to worship him
    as Lord of all,
    to have no gods before him,
    their thrones must fall.

Words and music: Graham Kendrick

JESUS IS THE NAME WE HONOUR

Jesus is our God

Brightly

1. Je - sus is the name we hon - our;

Je - sus is the name we praise.

Ma - jes - tic Name a - bove all

o - ther names, the high - est heav'n and earth pro-claim that

Je - sus is our God. *Refrain* We will

glo - ri - fy, we will lift him high, we will give him hon - our and praise. We will glo - ri - fy, we will lift him high, we will give him hon - our and praise.

2. Jesus is the name we worship;
   Jesus is the name we trust.
   He is the King above all other kings,
   let all creation stand and sing
   that Jesus is our God.

3. Jesus is the Father's splendour;
   Jesus is the Father's joy.
   He will return to reign in majesty,
   and ev'ry eye at last will see
   that Jesus is our God.

Words and music: Philip Lawson Johnston

I WORSHIP YOU, ALMIGHTY GOD

Words and music: Sondra Corbett

JESUS, JESUS

Holy and anointed one

Words and music: John Barnett

JESUS, WE ENTHRONE YOU

Je - sus, we en - throne you,

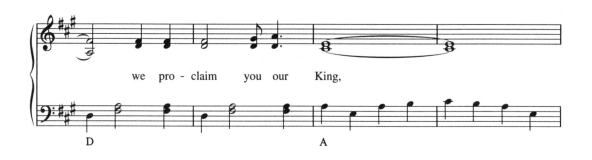

we pro - claim you our King,

stand-ing here in the midst of us,

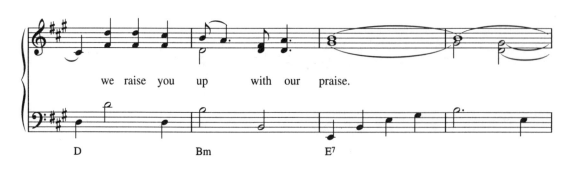

we raise you up with our praise.

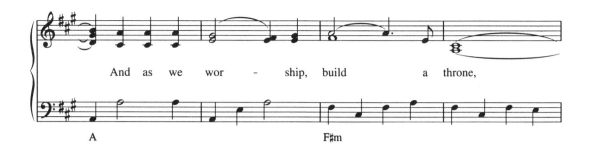

And as we wor - ship, build a throne,

A   F#m

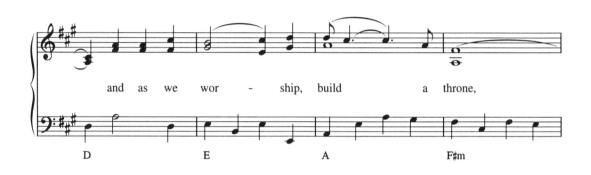

and as we wor - ship, build a throne,

D   E   A   F#m

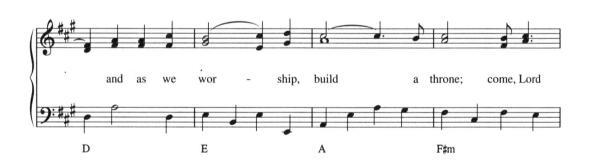

and as we wor - ship, build a throne; come, Lord

D   E   A   F#m

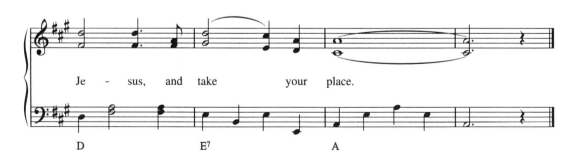

Je - sus, and take your place.

D   E⁷   A

Words and music: Paul Kyle

LORD, YOU HAVE MY HEART

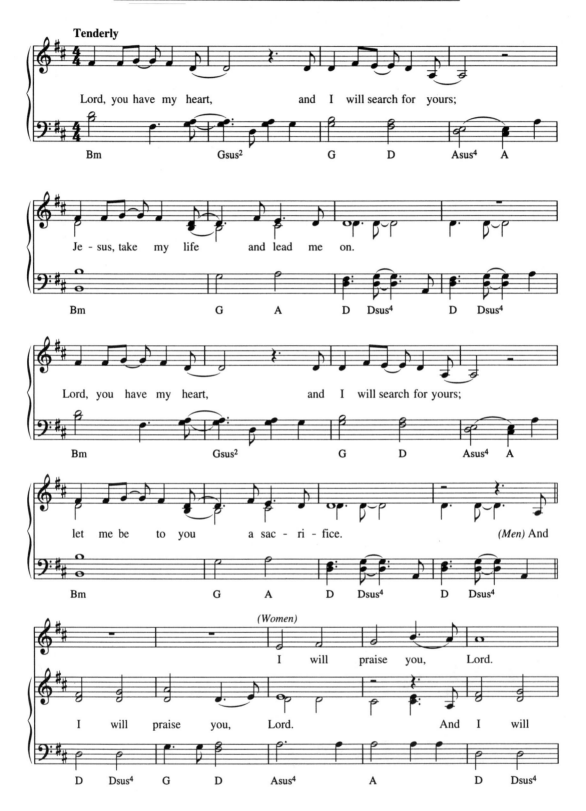

Words and music: Martin Smith

SPIRIT OF THE LIVING GOD

Spi - rit of the liv - ing God, fall a - fresh on me.

Spi - rit of the liv - ing God, fall a - fresh on me.

Melt me, mould me, fill me, use me.

Spi - rit of the liv - ing God, fall a - fresh on me.

* Capo 3

* Alternative capo chords for guitar

Words and music: Daniel Iverson

HE IS EXALTED

Triumphant

He is ex - al - ted, the King is ex - al - ted on high, I will praise him.

He is ex - al - ted, for - e - ver ex - al - ted, and I will praise his

name. He is the Lord, for - e - ver his truth shall

reign. Hea - ven and earth re - joice in his ho - ly name.

He is ex - al - ted, the King is ex - al - ted on high.

Words and music: Twila Paris

BY YOUR SIDE

Tenderly

By your side I would stay;

Bbmaj7   Cm7   F   Bb
* Capo 3 Gmaj7   Am7   D   G

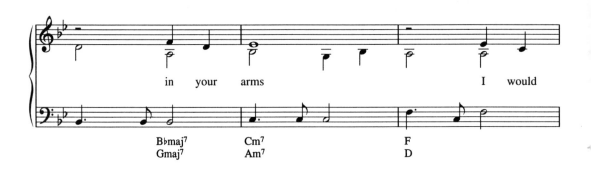

in your arms I would

Bbmaj7   Cm7   F
Gmaj7   Am7   D

lay.   Je - sus, lo - ver of my

Bb   Eb   Bb   Cm7   Bb
G   C   G   Am7   G

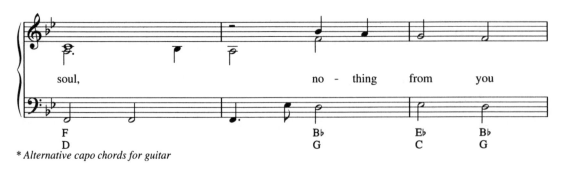

soul,   no - thing from you

F   Bb   Eb   Bb
D   G   C   G

* Alternative capo chords for guitar

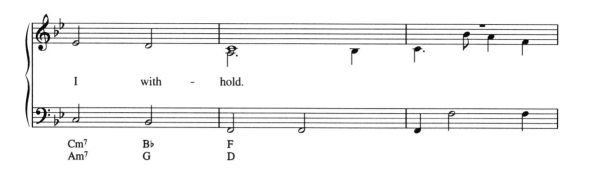

I with - hold.

Cm⁷ B♭ F
Am⁷ G D

Lord, I love you, and a - dore you; what more can I

E♭ B♭ Cm⁷ F
C G Am⁷ D

say? You cause my love to grow strong - er

B♭ E♭ B♭
G C G

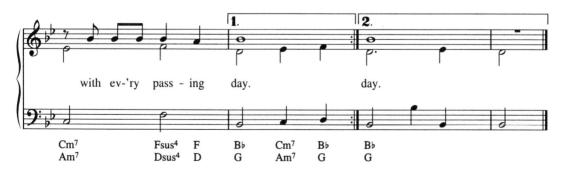

with ev-'ry pass - ing day. day.

Cm⁷ Fsus⁴ F B♭ Cm⁷ B♭ B♭
Am⁷ Dsus⁴ D G Am⁷ G G

Words and music: Noel and Tricia Richards

MY LIPS SHALL PRAISE YOU

Restorer of my soul

With energy

My lips shall praise you, my great Re -

* Capo 3

deem - er; my heart will wor - ship,

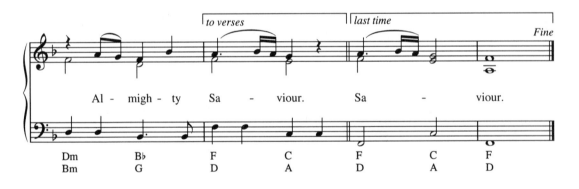

Al - migh - ty Sa - viour. Sa - viour.

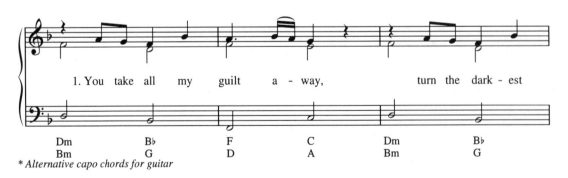

1. You take all my guilt a - way, turn the dark - est

* Alternative capo chords for guitar

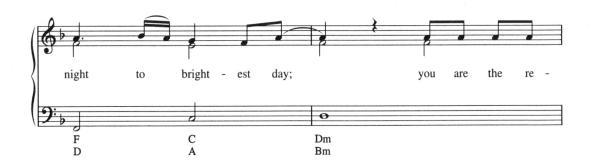

night to bright - est day; you are the re -

F C Dm
D A Bm

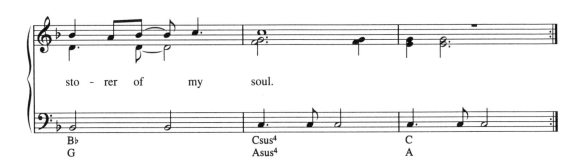

sto - rer of my soul.

Bb Csus⁴ C
G Asus⁴ A

2. Love that conquers ev'ry fear,
   in the midst of trouble you draw near;
   you are the restorer of my soul.

3. You're the source of happiness,
   bringing peace when I am in distress;
   you are the restorer of my soul.

Words and music: Noel and Tricia Richards

OVER THE MOUNTAINS AND THE SEA

I could sing of your love for ever

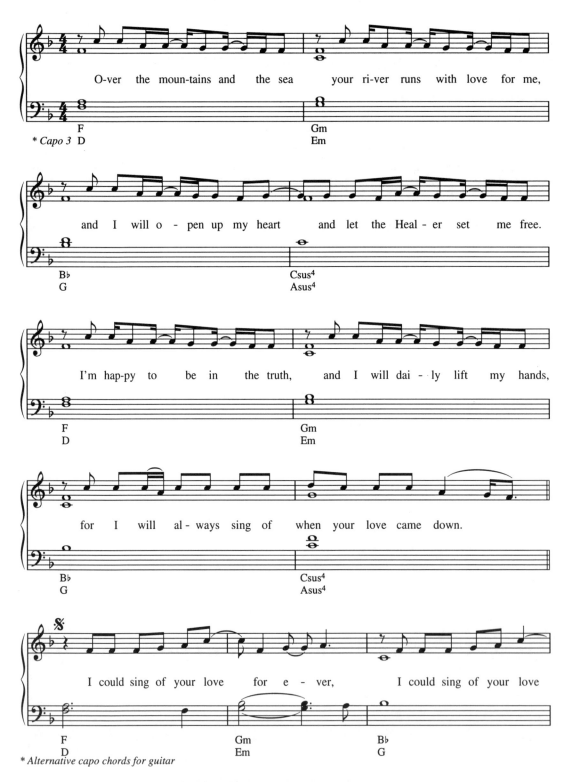

* Alternative capo chords for guitar

Words and music: Martin Smith

HE IS THE LORD

Show your power

1. He is the Lord, and he reigns on high; he is the Lord. Spoke into the darkness, cre-a-ted the light. He is the Lord. Who is like un-to him, ne-ver-end-ing in days; he is the Lord. And he comes in pow-er when we call on his name. He is the Lord.

Refrain

Show your pow - er, O Lord our God, show your God, our

God. 2. Your gos-pel, O Lord, is the hope for our na - tion; you are the Lord. It's the pow - er of God for our sal-va-tion. You are the Lord. We ask not for ri-ches, but look to the cross; you are the Lord. And for our in-he-ri-tance give us the lost. You are the Lord.

Refrain

Send your pow - er, O Lord our God, send your God, our God.

Words and music: Kevin Prosch

85